S0-DUH-263

Teaching Young Children
to Swim and Dive

Teaching Young Children to Swim and Dive

Virginia Hunt Newman

Photographs by Robert Newman

 Harcourt, Brace & World, Inc., New York

ALSO BY VIRGINIA HUNT NEWMAN

Teaching an Infant to Swim

Copyright © 1969 by Virginia Hunt Newman

All rights reserved. No part of this publication may be reproduced
or transmitted in any form or by any means, electronic or mechanical,
including photocopy, recording, or any information storage and
retrieval system, without permission in writing from the publisher.
First edition
Library of Congress Catalog Card Number: 72-76370
Printed in the United States of America

I dedicate this book to Mother,
who remembers:

"Mother dear," said little Gin,
"Today I'll help you all I kin,
but first I must go out to swim!"

Preface

This book has been written for young teachers and parents to help them teach swimming to children in the age group from five to seven. It concerns the "dog paddle," and the Australian crawl and the backstroke in their simplest forms. It also covers jumping and a plain front dive. Perhaps you have read my first book, *Teaching an Infant to Swim*. If so, you'll know how valuable I feel it is for children to learn how to swim as soon as possible—not only for the obvious reason of the child's safety in and around water, but because the activity of swimming will open up to him a lifetime of health and enjoyment in the water.

Most young swimmers don't go on to become athletic competitors, so I have purposely *not* gone into laborious detail; children in this age group are not ready for detailed instruction. The goal we strive for is to develop simple basic strokes without concern for perfection, but avoiding major bad habits that will have to be corrected later. Namely, rolling completely over on the side while breathing; pulling the arms down too fast and too soon, which makes it impossible to have a well-co-ordinated and smooth stroke; or "bicycling" the legs in the crawl. By the same token, we are not interested in how much the child bends his knees when he kicks, or whether he puts his fingers together and cups his hands when he strokes. These and other minor details constitute a later discipline: coaching—and there is a vast difference between teaching and coaching. Teaching merely means that you show the child how to swim, whereas coaching is training plus teaching—with great attention to detail. Here we shall be concerned with teaching.

There are reasons for teaching swimming in this manner. Perhaps the most important is that if you make the lessons too difficult, your pupils will begin to dislike swimming and will stop wanting to learn.

The child who stays interested in swimming will find many Red Cross programs that he can participate in, such as earning certificates for acquiring the various skills. Later, when he is older, he can earn Junior and Senior Lifesaving Certificates. Girls, particularly, often become interested in synchronized swimming, and can enter various water shows that are staged in public pools throughout the country each summer. Many teen-agers who are qualified get summer jobs as life guards and swimming teachers. So you see that even those who don't go on to become champions can gain many benefits from swimming.

If you let each child develop his own natural stroke, swimming will be much easier for him to learn. And if you look back in swimming history you'll find that the really great champions (Johnny Weissmuller and Eleanor Holm, for example, and the many others who followed) had their own unique way of swimming, suited to their own body builds. And even though most children don't become competitors, what's wrong with their swimming in the way that is most natural for them, just like the champions? (This principle, of course, is true in all sports. As an example: The great out-fielder Willie Mays has a unique way of catching the ball with both hands held out like a basket, although everybody who knows anything about baseball knows this isn't any way to catch a ball!)

My good friend Dr. Sammy Lee, who became one of the all-time great Olympic divers, has a short muscular body that lends itself to quick and complicated maneuvers which in turn have enabled him to master very difficult dives. When he first entered competition he was graded down by judges who snorted, "This is tumbling, not diving!" However, he became responsible for making diving the individual sport it is today, emancipated from being just a stepchild of swimming. As our teen-age son, Eddie, and his friends say, "Do your own thing."

Actually, what we are interested in in this age group is a natural, smooth stroke, without too much splashing or undue effort, and the formation of good basic habits which pave the way for future improvement.

Keeping these things in mind, follow the book step by step. You'll have children who not only have good strokes, but who like the whole activity well enough to go on to other swimming programs. And if you have a youthful swimmer who wants to compete —he'll be ready to be coached.

Contents

Teaching Young Children
to Swim and Dive

1

Introduction

Children accept life as it is presented to them—as good, or bad, or somewhere in between.

Learning to swim can be an exciting adventure or a frustrating and unpleasant experience. Whichever it is depends largely upon the teacher.

OPTIMUM CONDITIONS FOR LEARNING

A child will respond to swimming eagerly or fearfully, in exact accordance with the way it has been presented to him.

I've seen a child's swimming lessons become sheer torture because of the actions of an instructor who apparently couldn't care less about his pupil's welfare. Mostly, such teachers are young college students who have a summer job—that job for the moment being to teach swimming. Whether or not their little charges enjoy learning to swim is not taken into account.

3

Sometimes a mother scares her child by telling him that if he doesn't learn to swim he will drown. But a small child has no real understanding of the word "drown"; he only knows that it is something horrible. He is then often afraid that this "something horrible" will happen to him if he is in the water.

The experience of learning to swim should be fun, and a child should look forward to swimming lessons. This, of course, doesn't mean that he shouldn't have a healthy respect for the water or that he shouldn't start learning about safety around the pool.

A child's attitude about swimming is formed by his parents and his teacher.

Children in the age group I am going to discuss in this book—ages five through seven—don't need to have lessons as frequently as infants do. In the first place, they learn many skills just by playing in the water on their own. Also, when they are learning a definite skill such as moving their arms properly, they get bored if they are made to work too frequently—every day, for instance. As a result, they won't really try as hard as they would if they had lessons three times a week. (Not that they shouldn't play in the water every day if they want to.) I've seen many children who were excellent swimmers but didn't particularly like the water because they had to have a lesson every time they went in. Swimming to them just meant work, not fun.

For the same reason, a lesson should not exceed thirty minutes. And in my opinion twenty minutes is the optimum length of time for a child to get the most out of a lesson.

Children often learn more easily and have more fun if they take lessons in groups instead of privately. For one thing, they readily imitate one another. Although a teacher can demonstrate a skill, a child will more readily identify with someone in his own age group who has already achieved it, and will be more willing to try

4

an activity that looks difficult. A beginner gets discouraged if he can't perform as expertly as the teacher, but the discovery that he can perform just about as well as his peers in the group encourages him to go on trying.

There are also many games children can play as a group to help learn new skills and develop old ones. Such games are just another way of presenting swimming lessons—a way that contains built-in fun.

It is important that the temperature of the water be comfortable. A child may have difficulty in concentrating on the work at hand if he is too cold or too warm. For example, we learn many new skills with greater ease if we can perform them in slow motion,

To be a good teacher, you must not only teach your pupil to swim, you must develop the inborn love of water he had when he came to you.

because we get a better mental picture of what we are doing. But it is difficult to swim slowly in very cold water. On the other hand, it is sickening and not refreshing at all to swim in water that is too warm.

WHAT MAKES A GOOD TEACHER?

To begin with, and perhaps surprisingly, you don't have to be an excellent swimmer yourself to be a good teacher. Some of the worst teachers I have ever seen have been Olympic swimming champions. I learned to swim from an instructor who couldn't even swim herself. So George Bernard Shaw's maxim "He who can, does. He who cannot, teaches" is often true.

There's something much more important than swimming well yourself: *I think you must like children!* I've seen an instructor trying to teach a small child to swim when it was obvious that he couldn't stand him. Such an instructor doesn't do a good job even though he may succeed in teaching the child to swim. A good rapport hasn't been established between them, so the child doesn't enjoy his lessons and may actually come to hate the water. To be a satisfactory teacher you must not only teach your pupil to swim, you must help develop the inborn love of water he had when he came to you.

The next important qualification is to be able to make the child understand what it is you want him to do. You do so either by demonstrating yourself, or by having someone demonstrate for you, the skill you are trying to teach.

You'll find—particularly in this age group, which hasn't had much experience in organized learning—that there are some children who just don't pay attention. This is especially true when they've learned a little bit and all they want to do is play. So it

6

sometimes takes more time for you to get through to them than it does for them to master the skill once you actually have gotten through.

I had one such little boy at Black-Foxe Military School. He had been to three different schools, had received swimming instruction at each—and still couldn't swim. The first day of class we divided the group into swimmers and nonswimmers. The nonswimmers were to stay at the shallow end of the pool; I asked those who could swim to dive or jump into the deep water and swim across the pool so I could put them in groups according to their ability. Mark jumped into the deep water and started spluttering and was in apparent trouble, so I plunged in—clothes and all—to get him. When I pulled him to the edge and asked what was the matter, he said, "I can't swim!"

"What did I tell the nonswimmers to do?" I asked him.

And he didn't know because he hadn't been paying attention.

From then on, I tried to make sure, whenever I explained anything to the group, that Mark knew what I was talking about. If I did get through to him, he was usually in the top of the group for that lesson. And he was a delighted little boy when he finally became a successful swimmer. At least once a day he'd run up to me and say, "Gee, Ginny, I'm sure glad you made me learn to swim!" Then he'd go happily away and dive into the pool.

PROVIDING AN INCENTIVE

It's up to the teacher to provide or create an incentive. By the time a child is water safe, he often isn't interested in learning any more about swimming: he just wants to play. A reward in the form of a gift, a certificate, a ribbon, or something of the sort is a wonderful incentive for long-range progress. I use a toy gumball machine, and everyone who pays attention to the lesson and really tries gets a penny for gum.

Ginny's first law: No lesson—no gum!

TEACHING BY DISTRACTION

Sometimes a child will not want to try a skill because he thinks it's too hard or because he is a little leery of the consequences. (I'm talking here about apprehension, not about deep-seated fear, which we'll take up in a later chapter.)

A method that is often useful here might be called "teaching by distraction." As an example: The mother of a five-year-old called and said her little girl had been taking swimming lessons from another teacher, but was quite unhappy about them. Apparently Adrianna hadn't wanted to put her face in the water (the most common of all complaints about beginners in this age group) and after several unsuccessful attempts at coaxing, the teacher had started forcibly ducking her under the water. Each lesson then became an exercise in hysterics. I told the mother I'd see what I could do.

Adrianna had her swimsuit on when she met me at the door, and she promptly asked, "Are you a swimming teacher?" I said, "No, I'm your new friend, and I came to play with you in the pool." "Well," she said, "I won't put my face in the water!" I realized this wasn't going to be easy, but I assured her that she didn't have to do anything she didn't want to.

She readily went into the pool, and I carefully avoided getting too close to her so that she wouldn't think I was going to grab her and duck her head under the water. We started walking through

8

Learning to swim should be fun.

the water; first forward, then backward, turning around and just generally moving about. In the meantime I asked about her dog, her playmates, and even what she was doing in kindergarten. I heard someone observing say, "This is a swimming lesson?"

We continued, and after fifteen minutes or so of establishing a rapport I suddenly went under the water and came up saying, "Oh, Adrianna, I saw your pretty swimsuit under the water." I continued to go under and report what exciting things I had seen—a fish, a frog, and so on. Adrianna soon became so excited and curious that she just had to enter the game. So she started going under the water and telling me all the things she saw: "A whale, and a shark —and a great big octopus!" I had won her over. It was smooth sailing from then on.

As the renowned writer of sales-technique manuals Elmer Wheeler has said: "Don't sell the steak—sell the sizzle!"

WHAT SHOULD THE SWIMMING TEACHER WEAR?

The answer to that question may seem pretty obvious, but let me say in all seriousness that a swimming teacher ought to *look like a swimming teacher.* I've seen a young girl trying to get and hold the attention of a class while wearing a bikini, ignoring as best she could the whistles and wisecracks of young men going by. Small children are easily distracted, and also reflect anything that distracts the teacher. They also love to pick up and echo wisecracks.

So wait to wear the bikini until some occasion when you can privately enjoy the whistles.

In fact, I learned that a two-piece swimsuit has other ways of leading to an embarrassing experience. During World War II, when I was competing in diving, the U.S.O. sent us around to camps and hospitals to give water shows for servicemen. One weekend we got a "hurry-up" to go to El Mirador Hotel in Palm Springs, which had been temporarily converted into a hospital. My diving suit was at the Los Angeles Athletic Club and was to be brought to me before the show. As luck would have it, my suit was forgotten, and the only suit I had was a two-piece that I had brought along for sun-bathing. My coach, Bill Shaw, told me to go ahead and dive in it. Every time I went into the water the top came off, and I had to stay down at the bottom until I could get it back on. After the show I found out there was a subterranean room with a large window giving a perfect underwater view of the entire pool. And about twenty servicemen patients had congregated to watch my diving performance from this vantage point! I have always felt those guys weren't as sick as they were supposed to be. Anyway, I've had an aversion to two-piece suits ever since.

Men teachers don't have such problems with suits, but they should be careful about wearing kooky-looking garb such as big hats or sunglasses or white grease on their noses. Since men are so much bigger than small children, and have deep voices, they can easily seem like intimidating monsters and scare the kids half out of their wits.

CONCLUSION: SOME BASIC POINTS

I'd like to return here to that essential factor in successful teaching: *Be sure that a child knows what it is you want him to do.* Explain what you want not just so that he understands but in a way that he *cannot misunderstand.*

When our Ed was a little guy, about six years old, we lived next to a family with five children; being an only child, he enjoyed playing there. Once when they were away from home, he kept insisting that he wanted to go over to see if they had come back yet. I knew they still weren't home, but I finally gave in, after admonishing him, "Be sure to knock!" When he hadn't returned after ten minutes I went to find him. The door was open, and there was Ed in the playroom. I said, "Eddie, I told you to knock!" He looked at me, puzzled, and said, "I did, Mommy. I knocked." Sure enough, he had obeyed, but what I hadn't added was, "Don't go in the house if no one answers your knock." You can't assume that children will know what you mean unless you tell them exactly.

Be reasonably sure the child is physically capable of performing a skill before you ask him to attempt it. I've seen teachers trying to explain the backstroke to children who couldn't properly float on

11

their backs. It was frustrating for both the students and their teacher. If possible, don't put your pupil in a position of failing. He may get so discouraged that he will stop trying, and perhaps not want to try any further skills that are presented to him.

If he does fail, be sure to encourage him to try again. For instance, when you teach diving, if he can't get his foot up high enough to go in the water correctly, just say, "That's pretty good—you *almost* did it!" *Reward and praise are the key to good teaching.*

As you can see, a teacher benefits from having a number of special capabilities. Not the least of these is the ability to be a bit of a con artist when necessary.

2
Parents as Teachers

How about parents teaching their own children to swim?

Many parents think they may be incapable of doing so, even if they are very good swimmers themselves. But this is not necessarily true, and the parents I've been able to convince have had great fun and have been surprised at how easy it really is. The point is, anybody can be the child's swimming teacher for a reasonable length of time, a reasonable number of days a week.

The first and most important rule for parents to follow is *don't be his swimming teacher twenty-four hours a day*. This is where I think most parents fail in trying to teach their own children *anything*. Set aside the lesson time—two or three times a week—just as you would if he were going to a professional. The length of each lesson should not exceed thirty minutes. Then, when a lesson is not in session, don't try to instruct him. Even if you see him doing something wrong, keep your mouth shut. Wait until the next lesson to show him what he did or is doing that is wrong. It would be a good idea, psychologically, for you to have a special swimsuit that you use only for his lessons. When you wear it, you're his swimming teacher; when you change it, you stop teaching!

The above procedure will take a bit of discipline on your part, but, believe me, it's the only way—particularly if you have your own pool or live by a lake or at the shore, and see him in the water constantly. If you break the rule, he will soon feel you are nagging him, and he won't pay attention to you at any time. If you treat him as though you are a professional teacher, he will act accordingly.

If you succeed in enforcing such a schedule, you'll find that it is a lot easier to give him a lesson yourself than to get both of you dressed and drive several miles, and it's a heck of a lot cheaper.

The second rule—and it's almost as important as the first—is to *remember that you aren't training him for the Olympic Games.* Don't pick on every tiny little thing that he does wrong. Judge him on his own all-round ability, according to his age and experience. Approach the lessons with the attitude that he is learning for fun and safety and that you are having as much fun teaching him as he is having learning. After all, if he does turn out to be one in a million, and shows special interest and ability, you can always get a good coach later on.

Now that you have these basic points in mind, you're ready to begin. So, follow the book carefully, step by step, using your own good judgment. You'll be happily successful.

3

The Beginning Lessons

You'll find that teaching swimming, or anything else for that matter, is much easier if you take the time to get acquainted with your pupils and let them get acquainted with you. You'll also make it easier for all concerned if you explain to the children what you expect of them and what they are going to learn. You'd be surprised how many children don't know the names of the strokes, even though they may be excellent swimmers.

Before they get in the water, they should be told some of the things they should not do around the pool, such as pushing other children in the water, and why. Children in the age group we are dealing with are very much aware of their surroundings and should be taught proper poolside behavior. (For detailed suggestions, see Chapter 8.)

But—how do we get started with the early lessons? Here's one way I do it. At the beginning of the first lesson I tell them my whole name, and then I tell them that they may call me "Ginny." Next I tell them about my family and let them ask me questions about myself if they want to. At this point I am no longer a stranger to them, but a friendly swimming teacher. After each child has told us his name, and we are all acquainted, we proceed with the lesson.

GETTING USED TO THE WATER

To help the children get used to the water, I first have them sit on the edge of the pool dangling their feet and then kicking. This is at the shallow end, for obvious reasons. It will take about three minutes for them to get used to the temperature of the water. By then, they should be ready to go into the pool.

For safety's sake with beginners, it's a good idea to get in the water yourself or have an assistant get in the water with the children. Lined up in single file, each child in turn walks across the shallow end of the pool, along the edge. The first time across, some may want to hold onto the edge. When each child has made three or four trips across, have them walk across backward several times. The final formal activity for that day might be turning around in the water, first to the left and then to the right.

While all this is going on, it's fun for everyone to be singing. Most children in this age group like "Inky, Dinky Spider," which is a song I often use, but any favorite song of the group is fine.

In this first lesson, besides learning the rules of the pool, they have gotten the "feel" of moving in the water. Those of us who have been swimming a long time tend to forget that this is a strange feeling for anyone who isn't used to it. But used to it or not, they have also discovered that they're going to have a good time learning to swim!

16

Lined up single file, each child in turn walks across the pool, along the shallow end. Notice that Sean, who feels he isn't quite ready, sits on the edge watching.

After the formal part of the lesson it's playtime. In my opinion, playtime is almost as important as the lessons themselves. The children seize the opportunity to experiment on their own, inventing skills you would never think of teaching them. Providing a scheduled playtime also gives you a lever for control. Any child who disobeys you, or knowingly breaks a rule, simply does not get a playtime. You gain and keep control by rewarding good behavior. It's that simple. (Detailed suggestions for playtime activities will be found in Chapter 10.)

PUTTING THE FACE IN THE WATER

The first big hurdle to overcome after the child is used to being in the water is getting him to put his face under the surface. Some children will readily put their faces in the water, but for a great many of them, mostly girls, getting their faces wet is a big problem. Perhaps this reluctance stems from the fact that most mothers won't let their little girls get their hair wet when they take a bath unless it's going to be shampooed. If you've ever tried to get a heavy mop of long hair dry at 7:00 P.M. on a school night, you can understand why. (Boys, on the other hand, use a bathtub as a small swimming pool and are under the water more than on top, having a wonderful time. That is—until the soap arrives.)

This situation is unique; it's not a question of lack of ability or skill—nor is fear usually involved. Getting one's face wet is merely an uncomfortable feeling to some beginners, and it is overcome when they have had enough exposure to the water and enough experience in it. *A reluctant beginner should never be forced into putting his face in the water.* If you frighten your pupil by coercion, you will have two problems on your hands instead of one.

I've found that distraction is the easiest and fastest way to help your beginner over this hump, and that the best form of distraction is in games. One method is to have him look at his feet underwater, or perhaps pick up colored poker chips from the pool steps. Many times you can take advantage of an incident that comes up suddenly and unexpectedly. One little boy with whom I'd been having trouble was watching a group of boys play "Cops and Robbers" with pretend guns. As each kid was "hit" he fell over in the water "dead." I turned to Bruce, and, pointing my finger at him, said, "I got you!" He immediately took up the game and fell over in the water—head and all. And that hurdle was passed.

When I begin to suspect that the problem of getting his face in the water is going to present itself, I suggest that the child put his towel on the side of the pool close by so that he can dry his face each time he gets it wet. A child will often put his face in the water if he knows he will be able to dry it off immediately. Later on, as he becomes accustomed to having his face wet, he won't want the towel.

It may take several lessons for some children to become accustomed to a wet face, although this is the exception and not the rule. Children most often get used to the feeling simply by playing and splashing in the water. In any case, don't let your beginner proceed to the next step until he has mastered this one. (Unless fear is involved, a problem we'll discuss in Chapter 9.)

Three lessons at most should have brought him to this point, and in many cases he'll have reached it easily by the end of two. Now that he is familiar with moving about in the water and will put his face in, a cheerful game to add to the lessons is "Ring around the rosies."

Getting the face wet: a preliminary before submerging the face.

4

The "Dog Paddle"

Let me now go step by step instead of lesson by lesson. Some skills are harder to learn than others, and each pupil has already done some learning toward certain skills. Therefore, now aim to progress according to the ability of your pupils.

ARM MOVEMENT

Now that your pupil is comfortable moving about in the water, pay attention to his arms. As he walks across the pool, at shoulder depth, have him move his arms in a circling motion by reaching out his hands and then pulling them down toward his legs and on back. First one hand, then the other, rotating about each other like the pedals on a bicycle. The hands do not come out of the water. To make this exercise fun, I float plastic poker chips on the water for the child to pick up, using first the right hand, then the left. Here, then, is the arm stroke for the "dog paddle."

20

It just seems natural for children to start kicking when they are in the water.

KICKING

To teach the leg movement, or kick, is simple—because it just seems natural for a child to start kicking when he gets in the water. I have the child hold onto the top step while floating on his "tummy." Then I tell him to kick—after having demonstrated, of course.

We aren't going to be concerned here with "form." Most if not all beginners "bicycle" their legs when kicking. That action suffices at this point. Later, when we teach the crawl, we will develop the proper flutter kick.

SUSPENSION

This is the next step. Like moving about in the water, suspension without support is a most peculiar feeling. It's a new experience for beginning swimmers, and sometimes fear becomes involved. This is why I do *not* teach prone floating until the pupil can paddle about on his own. As a matter of fact, he usually discovers suspension himself during playtime.

To teach it, I use the following method: Hold the child by the waist with his face away from you, standing about three feet from the pool steps. Give him a slight push to the steps. He does not kick or move his arms, and probably won't put his face in the water. It doesn't really matter what he does, because the main purpose of this exercise is to get the feeling of suspension in the water without support. Repeat four or five times.

Pushing off into the water is a more difficult action psychologically for a child because he must initiate it himself.

Now, from the steps, he faces you and then pushes off into the water or falls over into it as you catch him. This is a more difficult action for him psychologically because he has to initiate it. Sometimes, if he hesitates too long, it is necessary for you to reach out and pull him gently off balance to get him started. Then give him a gentle push back to the step for the next try. If, up to this point, he hasn't put his face in the water when he's suspended, ask him to.

COMBINING KICKING AND ARM MOVEMENTS

When he becomes confident and feels at ease, move back a step or two before pushing him to the steps. Instruct him to kick his feet as he proceeds to the steps. This time as he pushes off to you he also kicks his feet.

You've guessed what comes next! The movement of the arms is added to the kick. By combining the action of arms and legs, he will be able to go farther. As he comes toward you, take several steps backward until he has taken four or five strokes. (It's not a good idea to stand too far away from the beginner at the start, because he doesn't realize how far he can swim and he won't try. Remember— don't put him in a position where he might be afraid or think he will fail.) Repeat three or four times. Now he is ready to see how far he can swim with your help.

Before you have him try it, first be sure to get his approval. I usually con him into it by saying, "Hey, that's so wonderful! How about seeing how far you can go? I'll help you! O.K.?"

When he has taken four or five strokes after pushing off from the steps, pick him up by the chin so that he can get a breath of air. Be sure that he has obtained a good breath, release him and let him

23

take three or four more strokes. Then pick him up again by the chin for air and release him again. When he is capable of swimming fifteen feet with your help, let him try to come up for air by himself.

This step sounds difficult, but it really isn't. Most children in this age group accomplish it on the first or second try. However, if a beginner has difficulty, try tapping him on the chin to get him started a couple of times; that usually does the trick. Encourage him to try to see how many times he can come up to get a breath and how far he can swim. But only in the shallow water. He's not ready for the deep water yet.

He should have reached this point in not more than four lessons, or two hours of water experience. That is, of course, if everything has been normal and there are no special problems of fear. Now you have a "beginner" swimmer, and the stroke he is using is commonly called the "dog paddle." (The Red Cross calls it the "human stroke." Technically, it's a crawl with a two-beat kick and underwater recovery of the arms.)

Don't turn up your nose at this stroke. Most people snub it because it's so easy. I guess they think you aren't really swimming unless you're using one of the formal strokes like the crawl or backstroke. Because it *is* so easy is the very reason it's the first thing I teach a child. Our primary concern, of course, is to ensure *early safety*. And here we have a simple stroke, easily learned in the first few lessons, that will make the child water safe while he is learning the more complicated and difficult strokes.

Facing: Here is the "dog paddle," a stroke that can be mastered easily with only two hours of water experience.

24

The fact that the dog paddle can be learned in a very short time encourages your young student to try harder during his lessons. Not only that, the dog paddle is fun! Children enjoy doing it, and it's a stroke they do not have to concentrate on to use. Learning the more difficult crawl too soon, without such a substitute, causes the child to get into bad habits, such as rolling too far to the side in stroking, which in turn results in a scissors kick instead of the correct flutter kick—because, of course, he swims any old way when he's not in class. These bad habits are later very difficult to overcome. The old saying "practice makes perfect" is all too true, and if you practice on the wrong thing you can wind up with a perfectly horrible stroke.

A beginning swimmer's dog paddle is somewhat akin to an infant's crawl before he walks. You can see how frustrating it would be if a baby were made to try to walk every time he wanted to get somewhere.

The dog paddle will allow the child to have a lot of safe fun in the water and help develop the co-ordination needed for the more difficult strokes, which he is now ready to attempt.

5

The Australian Crawl

Now that your pupil is water safe with the dog paddle, whether he learned it here or whether he has been swimming for several years, he is ready to learn the more complicated strokes.

The Australian crawl is the most common and popular of these, and certainly the fastest. It differs from the dog paddle in that the arms come *out* of the water in stroking, the kick is a faster flutter kick, and the head is turned to the side to breathe. The crawl is usually the· first formal stroke that is taught, and often the only one. Many adults feel that they're not really swimming unless they swim the crawl. I often hear, "Oh, I don't swim, I just sort of paddle around with the side stroke"—or breast stroke or whatever it is they use to propel themselves through the water. But, believe me, if they can save themselves from drowning they can swim, no matter what they call the stroke.

Children will have no difficulty learning a good crawl stroke if they have been prepared as your pupils have been. Before they start learning this stroke, or any other for that matter, I tell them what we are going to learn, and demonstrate the stroke so they will know what it looks like. Often I ask children, "Do you swim?" When they say, "Yes," I then ask, "Do you swim the crawl?" Most of the time their answer to me is, "I don't know—I just swim. What's the crawl?" I feel it's important for children to know what they are learning. It is certainly important for them to know what a stroke looks like before they start doing it. After all, children in this age group are still learning by imitation.

ARM MOVEMENT

The first step in actually teaching the stroke is to go back to walking across the pool and pulling with the arms. But this time, instead of making a half circle with them, we bring the arms out of the water and make a complete circle.

Start with both arms extended out straight, with the left hand on top of the right hand. The right hand pulls down through the water past the hip, then out of the water, and back to the starting position, but now on top of the *left* hand, making a complete revolution.

Repeat the motion, using the left hand. Continue the exercise, alternating arms. The pattern that the arms make is not a perfect circle but more like an oval. The arms are moved slowly, and one hand does not start the downward motion until the other hand is placed on top of it, so that each arm motion follows the same pattern. Evenness of motion will keep the beginner from going crooked in the water. Coming to this rest position also helps keep the hands from pulling too fast or too soon through the water, and will develop a nice smooth rhythm for the stroke.

This young girl
is demonstrating
the hand-over-hand
stroke as she walks
across the shallow
end of the pool.

"BALL-AND-SOCKET" ACTION OF THE SHOULDERS

It is important to move the arms slowly so the beginner can develop
the correct arm motion. The arms should be straight but not stiff.
The shoulders should be relaxed and square so that the arms will
move freely and independent of the shoulders. (I demonstrate here
how the ends of the arm bones slide in the socket of the shoulder if
the shoulders are relaxed. Making a fist with the right hand and
twisting it in the cupped palm of the left shows the pupil visually
how arm bones revolve in shoulder sockets if the shoulders are
relaxed.)

29

Practicing the arm movement should be included in each lesson, going four or five times across the pool, but not more than six. You must always remember that these children still have a rather short span of attention, and that you want to keep the lessons interesting and fun. As we learn the proper arm stroke, we also learn the proper kick for the crawl.

LEARNING BALANCE IN FLOATING

But before the swimmer can develop a good flutter kick, he must be able to float prone while being well balanced in the water. There is no particular skill attached to learning to float. In normal circumstances, if you merely demonstrate it to children they will imitate you. Often, in fact, you will find that your pupils have already taught themselves to float while playing in the water.

But balance is important in floating, and the trick to learning it is to *stretch*. To teach children to stretch while floating, I have them pretend that they're rubber bands and tell them to try to see how long they can make themselves. This is another example of teaching by distraction. A child will work much harder at pretending to be a rubber band than he would if you just told him to stretch.

After he feels at ease in the stretching-floating position, he's ready to add the flutter kick itself.

THE FLUTTER KICK FOR USE WITH THE CRAWL

While the children were learning the dog paddle, they used any kind of kick that came naturally to them. Usually it was a kick that involved "bicycling," or pedaling of the legs. But in the Australian crawl, where balance and timing are important, a good flutter kick is necessary.

One of the most common misconceptions about the flutter kick is that the legs are to be kept stiff and straight. "Don't bend your knees" is something I often hear. But it isn't that you must not bend your knees. You should. It's that you shouldn't bicycle them. Developing a good flutter kick is worth all the extra time it takes.

Demonstrate the kick to your pupils by slowly moving your own legs up and down, using the whole leg from the hip, as you yourself float prone. When your pupils try the kick themselves, be sure they move their legs from the hip. This will produce a very straight-legged stiff kick, which is what you want at the beginning.

After a couple of exercises of stretching and kicking, have them try *relaxing* and kicking. Alternating stretching and kicking with relaxing and kicking will help develop a nice natural kick. This alternating exercise will prevent or help overcome the bicycling of the legs that is, as I said, so common among beginners.

REVIEWING THE ARM STROKE

Meanwhile, the child should be continuing to practice the arm stroke. But now he should put his face in the water as he walks across the pool and makes the circles with his arms. If he moves them slowly, as he should, he will be able to take four or five strokes before he needs a breath of air.

However, this is *not* the time to teach him to breathe. Tell him that when he needs air, he should stop his arm motion, stand up straight, and inhale deeply before proceeding. When a beginner finds himself running out of air, he has a tendency to start flailing

She puts her face
in the water as she
moves her arms
and walks across
the pool.

his arms and kicking his feet rapidly, which in turn cause him to stroke improperly. Always keep in mind that you will not have to correct bad habits that don't exist.

COMBINING ARM AND LEG ACTION

By the time the child is capable of walking across the pool, moving his arms with his face in the water, and coming up for air a couple of times if necessary, he is ready to put the actions of the arms and legs together to make the whole stroke. To accomplish this, he first floats, then he kicks his feet, and lastly he starts his arms. We have here the rudiments of the Australian crawl.

When the child puts the arm and leg action together, he should be able to swim ten to fifteen feet before he needs a breath of air. But here again he should *not* try to take a breath while he is moving his arms; he will be breathing incorrectly and will tend to develop bad stroking habits. For example: A beginner, when trying to get a breath of air as he swims, will generally bring his head straight up out of the water as he does in the dog paddle. His feet go down, his shoulders come out of the water, and he is now not able to move his arms properly; his legs start bicycling. His stroke, in fact, completely disintegrates.

So, when it becomes necessary for him to get air, he should again stop stroking, stand up, and take a breath. The interruption also gives him a chance to rest his arms and legs, and to stop concentrating for a moment. When he goes back to swimming, he should start out fresh: first floating, then kicking, then stroking.

To repeat: In teaching the kicking and stroking skills, I have my pupils *practice each separately*. This gives them a chance to concentrate on each skill and thoroughly absorb it, so that when the two skills are put together they will be able to perform them automatically.

One way for pupils to have a good time with this exercise is to walk across the pool once just stroking, next trip cross it floating and kicking only, and on the third trip really swim across. Practicing in this way serves two purposes. First, of course, it develops the skills. But it also relieves the monotony of doing the same thing over and over. And it's rather fun to "pull one, kick one, swim one." At least, the kids think so.

The trick in learning to balance in floating is to stretch.

Now we add the kick to the stretching-floating position.

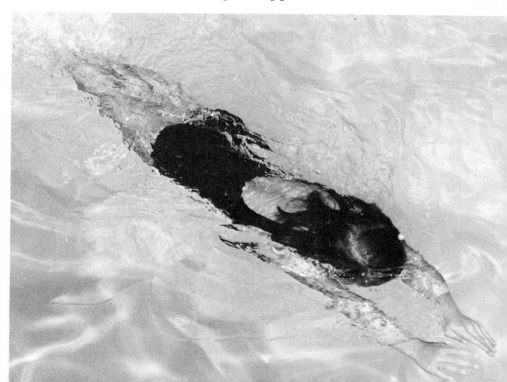

Here the student is relaxing and kicking while floating prone.

Now she combines the arm and leg action to make a whole stroke.

Up to this point we have been working on the "hand over hand" stroke, which I use to teach the crawl or to correct bad habits that have developed when swimmers have been taught improperly. Now it is time to progress to a more natural way of stroking.

We go back, first, to walking across the pool with the face out of the water and stroking as we did in the beginning lessons. But instead of each arm making a complete revolution independently or separately, one of them makes just a half circle before the other starts its motion.

Let's begin with the right hand. First it pulls down to the side. When it brushes by the right leg, the left hand begins to move down toward the left leg, and as the right hand goes around to make the full circle and come back to the original position, the left hand is moving down to the left leg. Then the right hand proceeds down and brushes by the right leg again while the left hand pulls around and comes back in a full circle to the original position.

In other words, each arm moves around in a circle but the arms are a *half circle* apart. In the beginning I have the children stop at each half stroke so that they can see what position each arm should be in at this point, and then proceed until they cross the pool. It usually doesn't take more than three or four trips across the pool for them to get the idea of the new stroke. Now we try it without stopping at each half stroke. Then we repeat with the face in the water, but still walking.

The next step is to try the new stroke with the kick. As before: first the float, then the kick, and then the stroke. I think you'll find that ninety-nine times out of a hundred your pupils will have pretty good form. These extra little steps in learning—the ones many people may think unnecessary—will have paid off!

36

Each arm moves
around in a circle,
but now the arms are
a half circle apart.

Notice here how her body is riding the water. By holding her chin up and keeping her head slightly above her body, she lets her legs go deeper into the water, which in turn gives her kick more power.

This series of pictures shows the path the arms take. Notice that as she strokes, her shoulders stay level and she doesn't roll from side to side. In the last picture notice how deep her kick is and notice also that although she bends her knees quite a bit, she doesn't "bicycle" her legs.

Your beginner should now have the experience and the co-ordination to learn to breathe. I generally wait four or five lessons after a student has learned the arm stroke before I start to teach breathing. You will find that if the student doesn't have to think too much about his arm stroke, it will be easier for him to concentrate on breathing. In turn, learning to breathe will be easier. You must remember that the breathing skill in the Australian crawl is the most difficult thing for beginners to learn.

Again, demonstrating is important. Go through the motions of breathing slowly so the beginners can see exactly what the arms and head do.

I usually start with a little exercise of having the child put his face in the water and rotate it from side to side so as to get the feeling of the head's motion. I tell him to choose which side he wants to learn to breathe on. After he has rotated his head several times, he decides which side *seems* easier. I say "seems" because it isn't always easy to tell, and a beginner will often change his mind. However, most people use the right side. I don't know why. I've found it hasn't anything to do with being left- or right-handed. It doesn't really matter which side one learns to breathe on, and when a swimmer becomes accomplished enough I teach him to breathe on either side alternately.

For simplicity, let's assume that the beginner has chosen to learn on the right. Standing, the pupil goes back to stroking his arms with his face in the water. His left hand is extended out in front of his body as though he were about to start a new stroke. His right hand is extended back and is touching the side of his leg, as if it had just pulled through the water. It is at this point that he turns his head to the right, while his left hand remains extended. He turns his head until his whole mouth is out of the water, and takes a breath by opening his mouth and inhaling.

After inhaling, he turns his head back, puts his face in the water, and exhales through his mouth. (Some people think they should inhale through the mouth and exhale through the nose—that their mouths should be closed when their faces are in the water. However, it's easier to inhale and exhale through the mouth. Plus the fact that when exhaling through the nose, it is difficult to empty the lungs of stale air, which in turn causes fatigue and shortness of breath.) As he is turning his head, the left hand begins to pull down through the water and the right hand comes up over into position in front of the body to start a new stroke. This is the breathing procedure—simplified and in slow motion.

SPACING THE BREATHS

When the beginner is learning to breathe, he should *not* take a breath every stroke. In the first place, it's too difficult for him because he hasn't developed the co-ordination needed—and secondly, he's not swimming so far that he needs air that often. When a beginner tries to breathe at each stroke, he starts rolling over too far on his side when he turns his head; the first thing you know, he has the bad habit of pulling with just one arm (his so-called "breathing" arm) and the other just sort of paddles under his body. I know you've seen kids swim like this! Therefore, I encourage a student to take about four strokes between breaths. Breathing at every fourth stroke gives a beginner a chance to prepare himself mentally and physically so that when he does take a breath he will do it correctly.

Here is a series of pictures showing the mechanics of breathing. Notice that the left hand is in position, ready to stroke when she turns her head, and remains in position until her face is out of the water. Her hand pulls slowly down through the water as she gets her breath. Then her right hand comes around to stroke as she places her face back in the water.

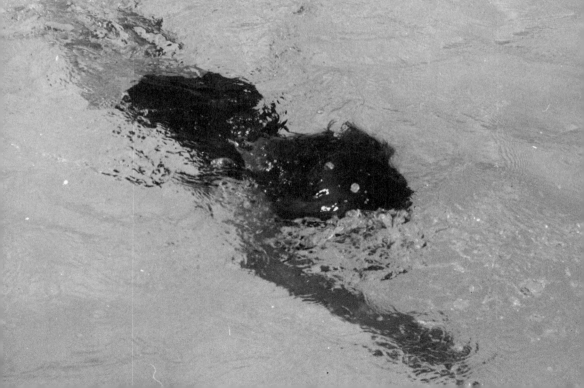

An experienced swimmer is capable of breathing any time he wants without changing his body position in the water. How often he breathes depends upon how fast and how far he is going. If he was swimming a short sprint of, say, fifteen yards, he probably wouldn't take a breath at all. But if he was swimming a mile or more, he'd breathe every stroke to keep fresh oxygen in his lungs.

COMBINING BREATHING AND SWIMMING

It usually takes five or six lessons before a student can breathe smoothly enough in his practicing to try it while he's swimming. Remember, this practice exercise takes up just a small part of the lesson. So give him plenty of time to breathe really properly before he attempts it while swimming.

When you feel that he is ready to put the breathing with the whole stroke, he should *not* start out by taking a breath with the first stroke. Instead, he should take several strokes to get in balance and gather some momentum before trying to turn his head. If he has any difficulty the first few times he tries, I usually walk along beside him and tap him on the head when the arms are in position for him to turn his head to the side. Remember that when he is swimming and breathing he is thinking of three things: his arm movements, his leg kick, and his breathing. So sometimes a little aid will make it easier for him to learn.

When he tries the breathing on his own, have him take just one breath. That is, he should take four strokes, then take a breath, then four more strokes, and then stand down to begin again. As he develops in co-ordination, and can breathe smoothly and evenly, it is time to add more breaths to the strokes. He still should not, however, customarily take a breath at each stroke until he is able to swim at least forty feet taking breaths at every fourth stroke.

When he has developed to the point where he can breathe well with every stroke—and this takes several months—I start teaching him to breathe on the opposite side. But a child in the age group we are considering doesn't have the co-ordination to breathe on both sides unless he has been swimming for several years.

The foregoing may sound unnecessarily complicated, but I have purposely gone into great detail so that the mechanics of the stroke can be understood.

A child ought to know exactly what the arms and legs and head are supposed to do, but he often learns this more quickly than my step-by-step directions may suggest. For instance, most children learn the hand-over-hand step in one lesson, and no child should need more than two. Often, when I see that a boy or girl is well co-ordinated, I skip the phase in which he stops at each half stroke. Other times, when a child has learned the stroke but starts slipping into bad habits, we go back and review each step.

You have to be the judge; but as long as a child is swimming smoothly, without rolling or splashing, he is on the right track.

6

The Backstroke

The backstroke is comparatively easy to learn because breathing doesn't become involved as it does in the crawl. Before he begins the backstroke, though, the child needs to know how to float on his back. (As I mentioned earlier, I really have seen teachers trying to teach a child the backstroke before he could even float properly.) So be *sure* first that the young swimmer can float easily and with balance.

FLOATING ON THE BACK

I think the most common problem here is that in trying to float most children "pike," or "sit down in the water" with their faces submerged. (After you've spent a lot of time trying to get them to put their faces in the water, now you have to spend a lot of time trying to get them *not* to put their faces in the water!) But once a child gets the knack of putting and *keeping* his head back, floating on his back is a relatively easy skill for him to learn.

He starts by holding onto the edge of the pool with knees drawn up in a *tuck* position. With the head held back, he lets go of the edge and unfolds onto the water, *keeping his head back.* It is very important that he *not* push away from the side. Pushing only causes him to go under the water. (This rule applies only to a beginner learning to float on his back. When he has learned the skill well, he will have better control, and can push from the edge without going under.)

In trying to float on the back, most children "pike," or "sit down in the water" with faces submerged. This piking position makes it impossible to stroke the arms properly.

The pupil starts the back float by holding onto the edge of the pool with knees drawn up in a tuck position and head held back.

Now he lets go of the edge and unfolds onto the water, keeping his head back.

He must continue to hold his head back as he floats.

Here is an underwater picture of the proper position for back floating.

He must continue to keep his head back. He will probably tend to bring his head forward, submerging his face in the water, which in turn pushes his feet down. And you can't learn the backstroke in this position. If, after several tries, a beginner still pulls his head forward, I stand behind him as he unfolds and hold his head in position. Once he gets the feel of this position, I let him try again on his own. He is almost always successful the second time around. After he can float properly, we see how long he can float. First five seconds, then ten, then fifteen; some can float for as long as half a minute.

Now he is ready for the kick.

THE KICK

I have found that the simplest way to teach the mechanics of the kick is on the steps. Have the pupil sit on the steps with his legs extended out into the water. The legs should be slightly apart, with the toes pointed in and touching each other. The heels should be a couple of inches apart. It is common for a beginner to place the heels together, with the toes apart and not pointed. But to manage a good kick the legs *must* be in the proper position.

As the legs are extended, the kick starts with a slight bend of a knee—it doesn't matter which one, but I always suggest the right. Then, as the leg straightens, the foot kicks as though kicking a ball. Slowly kick in this manner, using first one leg and then the other; increase the speed as the beginner gets the "feel" of the kick. It should take only five minutes or so for him to learn the kicking skill. Although it may sound complicated, it's really rather easy for a child with normal co-ordination.

Before we combine the kick with the backstroke float, I usually

50

have the pupil kick while lying back and leaning on his elbows while still on the steps. This practice just makes it a little easier later to combine the kick with floating.

COMBINING FLOAT AND KICK

To put the kick together with floating, the beginner should first unfold from the edge, extending his legs out in a good position. Then he starts the leg motion slowly, speeding the kick as he is able.

A boy or girl with normal co-ordination should develop a good kick in two lessons. But however long it takes, he must have a good float and kick before he goes on to the arms, or he'll get into a lot of bad habits.

BODY POSITION

Another important contribution to a good backstroke is body position; and this, again, we learn by *stretching*. We add the stretching to the floating and kicking before we add the arm stroke.

Have the pupil begin again by holding onto the edge of the pool. As he lets go and unfolds to float, his hands go past his head and flatten out along the water behind him; with his arms straight, he makes his body as long as he can. (As I said earlier, sometimes children like to pretend they are rubber bands.) It may take a couple of tries before a beginner can get his arms up over his head and stretched properly. When he succeeds, we add the kick, slowly at first and then faster as he is able. The first thing you'll notice is how much better balanced he is in the water when he stretches.

Here he is stretching and kicking.

Moving both arms simultaneously at first will help to develop the correct backstroke pattern.

STROKING WITH THE ARMS

Now we add the arm stroke. This will be easier to learn if the child starts by moving his arms *simultaneously* in the backstroke pattern. (It is almost impossible to move the arms incorrectly when you move them together.)

Standing in the water, chest-deep, the child stretches his arms up over his head—a shoulder width apart, with the hands turned palms outward. It is very important that the palms be facing *away* from the body; they should *never* be pointed toward the body when the arms are out of the water. From their position over the head, the arms start a backward motion and make a full circle until they come back in place. This motion is not the correct arm pattern for the backstroke, but it helps the beginner get the feeling of moving his arms in the opposite direction from the one he uses in the crawl. In effect, this is just an exercise to help him get started.

One lesson is all it will take for him to get the feeling of moving his arms in this backward direction. Then we go to the exercise of moving one arm at a time. With the arms in position up over the head, the right arm moves in a full circle; then the left arm moves and makes the full circle around. These arm movements must be slow.

Now, as in the crawl, we progress to moving the arms so that they are a half circle apart. Start with the right arm: pull it down to the right side. As it starts the upward motion to finish the stroke, the left arm moves down to the left side; as the left arm comes up to finish the stroke, the right hand comes down to touch the side, and so on.

The backstroke resembles the crawl except that the swimmer is on his back and he is moving his arms in the opposite direction.

As he places his right hand in the water, the left hand pulls down to his side.

He keeps his arms to the side of his body in the backstroke so as not to splash water in his face.

It is important that the hands be placed in the water palms down.

COMBINING ARM ACTION WITH THE KICK

Now the arm action is added to the floating and kicking, making a whole stroke. We go back to the edge of the pool, unfolding, then kicking, then moving the arms—slowly, first the right arm, then the left. After a couple of lessons of swimming backstroke in this way, it's time to learn the correct path that the arms should take.

When the arms are brought up out of the water, they come out to the side of the body and move in a path up over the body, always staying to the side so that he will not splash water in his face. The arms remain straight and are placed in the water palms down a shoulder width apart above the head. It is important that the hands be *placed* in the water, not slapped into it. As the swimmer pulls his arms down through the water, he should keep reaching toward the end of the pool to get the full power of the stroke. The path of stroke when he puts his hand in the water is down straight to the side and does not go much beneath the body. The pulling of the arms in this manner prevents the body from rocking from side to side as the pupil swims.

Up to this point the beginner has been swimming very slowly so that he can learn the stroke properly. When you are satisfied that he is stroking to his own best ability, your pupil can speed up. While the pupil can always increase his speed as he progresses, he should try to do so without getting into bad habits. Remember that having a good stroke is important.

As in the crawl, I have gone into great detail, particularly concerning the arms, so that the child will have a good mental picture of what the arms are supposed to do. And here again, if the child is swimming smoothly, without splashing or slapping his hands in the water, he is probably swimming correctly.

56

7

Jumping and Diving

Most children teach themselves to jump into the shallow water by just being eager beavers about getting in, and jumping is the quickest and easiest way. But not so many are courageous enough to go jumping into water over their heads.

And diving, of course, is for the deep water only, so in this chapter we will concern ourselves especially with deep water. Naturally, then, the child must be a fairly good swimmer—having mastered at least the dog paddle.

JUMPING INTO DEEP WATER

Let's start with the child who isn't adventurous enough to try jumping by himself. It really is a simple thing to stand in the shallow end of the pool and hold the child's hand while he jumps into the water. After a couple of jumps he'll be able to go in by himself.

57

I'm talking about a child who is just not adventurous—not one who is afraid. Fear is a whole other subject, which we'll take up later. (See Chapter 9.)

So let's proceed to the deep water. Any water that is over the child's head is "deep"—but I usually go with him to the deepest part of the pool. I stand on the edge beside him, hold his hand, and jump in with him a couple of times. Then I stay in the water while he climbs out and jumps in alone. I take this precaution because it is a new experience for the child to be in water over his head.

Be sure to tell him to push off from the bottom of the pool so that he will ascend rapidly and not run out of air. A couple of jumps while I am in the water are usually all that is needed. Sometimes, of course, it is necessary to teach a child to jump into very deep water—over fifteen feet—in which it would be impossible for him to reach the bottom. He then must learn to find his way back up to the top without a push from the bottom.

USING A ROPE

I have found that a clothesline rope (or in a pinch a jump rope) is a great tool for teaching children to jump into such "bottomless" water—usually a lake or other natural body of water. If possible, the rope should be about fifteen feet long. Be sure to use a regular clothesline rope made of stranded cotton or nylon, not smooth plastic. The plastic cords are too slippery, and you get splinters in your hands if you use the ones made of hemp. If you use a jump rope, the child can hold onto the handle.

To use the clothesline, first tie a knot in each end of the rope, then coil it. Let the child have one end of the rope, wrapped once around his hand, and you hold the other. When he jumps in and descends, the rope unwinds. When he reaches the depth to which he is going (he'll begin to lose momentum and slow down), you merely pull him up to the surface. Not so slowly that he will run out of breath, but also not so fast that you'll frighten him. Children usually take this as a game.

After a couple of tries, encourage him to take the rope down, but to leave it there and come up by himself by kicking and pulling as he ascends. From this point it's an easy step to get him to jump in by himself without holding onto the rope. The first couple of times he tries on his own, I leave the rope in position for security. He knows it's there in case he wants to use it.

If you follow the simple steps I have outlined, your pupil will have effortlessly progressed to a new skill.

JUMPING FROM THE DIVING BOARD

Jumping from the diving board rather than from the edge of the pool takes a little more courage.

As before, I hold the child's hand a couple of times while he jumps. When he tries by himself you'll find he has a tendency to look down, which causes him to fall forward and sometimes land flat on his tummy—a "bellyflop." So I have him look at something straight ahead, such as trees in the distance, if we're outside, or perhaps a clock on the wall at the opposite end of the pool if we are inside. Most children, especially boys, will soon get up enough courage to jump from the diving board without assistance. The type of jumping we're discussing here is not the fancy kind con-

The pupil holds one end of the rope, which is wrapped around her hand, and you hold the other. She holds the rope as she jumps into the water. When she reaches the depth to which she is going, you merely pull her up.

nected with diving, in which you stretch and twist and tuck (that takes further skill), but just a simple, expedient way to get into the pool.

SIMPLE DIVES

Although it takes a little more boldness, simple diving is just as easy as jumping. In fact, in some ways it's easier than jumping because you can see where you're going.

I often tell the story of our little girl, Patty, who at eighteen months did a perfect dive just by imitating an older boy I was teaching. After watching us for several minutes she went to the edge of the pool, bent over with her head down, one leg extended and lifted behind her, and slithered into the water as though she had been practicing for days. Bigger children, in the five-to-seven age group, aren't so brave—they have better sense. However, demonstrating to them can help a lot.

A good way to teach a simple dive is to have the child put one foot (it doesn't matter which one, but if they ask I tell them the right one) at the edge of the pool with the toes curled over the edge and the leg slightly bent. The other foot is placed a foot or so directly behind, with the toes pointing away from the body. The body then bends deeply at the waist—it is *very* important that the body be bent deeply—with arms stretched out toward the water, and the head down. As the child loses his balance and falls forward, the rear foot comes up over his body and he enters the water head-first. It helps if you give him something to dive toward—such as the drain.

Three things are important here:
1. Keep the head down.
2. A deep body bend.

62

3. Keep the foot and leg over the head going into the water. The legs should not bend.

It seems easier for most kids to keep their heads down than to get their foot high enough. And they have to master this before they can go on to the next step, or they'll "bellyflop"—and that hurts.

Sometimes children are reluctant to enter the water headfirst. If they are guided into the water a couple of times, it will help them get the "feel" of diving.

Here the pupil puts her right foot on the edge of the pool, with toes curled over the edge and the leg slightly bent. The left foot is placed directly behind. The body bends deeply at the waist, with arms stretched out toward the water and the head down. As she falls forward, her left foot comes up over her body and she enters the water headfirst.

Sometimes, when a child tries and tries repeatedly but unsuccessfully to get his leg up high enough, he gets a mental block and then the right position seems impossible to him. In this case I have him try switching legs, bringing the other one up. This variation often enables him to break through his mental block.

One six-year-old boy was having difficulties and I said, "Matthew, try putting your other leg up once and see if that will help." And thinking, perhaps, that it would be even more difficult, he said, "Ginny, would you give this leg just one more chance?" I agreed, and with extra special effort he succeeded.

The double take-off dive: As she bends forward, losing her balance, she gives a push from the edge of the pool and points her hands to the bottom.

DOUBLE TAKE-OFF DIVE

Now, when your student is capable of a good "fall-in" dive he is ready to learn the *double take-off dive*. The double take-off dive merely means using *both* feet in pushing off from the edge of the pool. His feet should be a bit apart so that he can keep his balance. It also helps if he bends his knees slightly. As he bends forward, now losing his balance, he gives a push from the edge, points his hands to the bottom, and goes in.

Proper use of the arms comes next. He stands in the same position, but his arms are now at his side instead of over his head. As he pushes from the edge of the pool, his arms are thrust up over the head into a position pointing to the bottom of the pool.

DIVING OUT INTO THE WATER

As he becomes proficient in diving down deep, I start teaching him to dive *out* into the water instead of down into the water. This is accomplished by aiming the head and arms out and diving toward the opposite end of the pool. This is an undeveloped racing dive. (Children in this age group, especially boys, like to race among themselves and are anxious to learn a racing dive.)

In terms of his own best ability in this age group, your student has now mastered a *plain forward dive*.

Starting with the arms back, she pushes from the edge of the pool. Her arms are then thrust up into a position pointing to the bottom of the pool.

8

Safety First

Learning to be safe in and around water must be an integral part of learning to swim.

Many of the accidents and tragedies that occur near the water are the result of either ignorance or carelessness. Many times the water is not at all to blame—dangerous conditions can be just the result of sheer stupidity. For instance, I once knew a man who was so determined that his young children wouldn't drown that he drained all the water out of his pool. Then he let them ride around the edge of it on their bikes!

The most common cause of water accidents to otherwise strong and competent people is the cocky attitude of some very good swimmers who feel that they are not bound by rules. But many excellent swimmers—and even champions—have drowned because they didn't obey some of the simple basic rules of safety.

It is never too soon to start teaching safety. Probably one of the first rules students should be taught is *never to swim alone*. A body of cool water on a hot day looks mighty inviting to a young child. Unless he is taught in no uncertain terms that it is dangerous, he may very well go into the water alone, particularly if he knows how to swim. He should be taught *from the beginning* that he will never become so good a swimmer that he cannot drown—no one does. (I don't mean to scare the child, just instill a healthy respect for the water. Sudden cramps, momentary blackouts from bumped heads —many minor mishaps can become sources of danger unless other swimmers are present.)

As a matter of fact, most of the safety rules for children are "don'ts." And I feel that it is necessary to teach them why. For instance, a child might not realize that he shouldn't dive in shallow water because he could injure himself if he hit the bottom of the pool—unless he's had personal experience. And, believe me, it's not much fun to learn the hard way when it comes to safety.

Following is a list of safety rules to be taught—and why:

Don't push anyone into the water. Just because a person is standing by the edge of the water (even deep water) doesn't mean he can swim. Even if the person being pushed *can* swim, in trying to catch himself from falling he may easily hit the edge and injure himself.

Don't run! This rule is so obvious I generally ask the children to tell me why they shouldn't run. (One five-year-old said, "Well, if you run your mother spanks you.") Most surfaces are slippery when wet. And it's almost impossible to keep the areas around a pool dry.

Be sure the way is clear before you dive or jump into the water. This goes for the edge of the water as well as the diving board. By the same token, after a jump or dive the beginner should be taught to get out of the way for the next person to enter the water.

Don't duck anyone or hold onto anyone in the water. As a matter of fact, I've made a rule that children shouldn't even touch each other unless they're playing tag or some other game under supervision.

Use such accessories as slides in a safe way. As far as slides go, the same safety rules apply as on the playground, with the added hazard of the water.

Jump straight out into the water. When jumping into the water, children—particularly beginners—often will turn as they jump and catch onto the side. This way of jumping is very hard on chins, teeth and noses. The same goes for jumping and diving from a corner and trying to catch onto the side of the pool.

The diving board is a special danger if improperly used. Children should not double-bounce on the end of the board unless they are taking instructions and are under supervision.

Many accidents occur when swimmers swim under diving boards while they are being used. In some locations, special diving wells are now being built that are separate from pools used for swimming.

Kick-boards can be very hazardous if used carelessly. They shouldn't be thrown, and they shouldn't be stood on, especially near the edge of the pool.

LAKES AND RIVERS

Swimming at the shore, in lakes, and in rivers presents other problems. There are often roped-off areas for swimmers. It shouldn't be assumed that children will stay within these boundaries. They should be shown the boundaries and *told* to stay within them. If the area is not roped off, children should be shown a point beyond which they should not swim.

BOATS AND CANOES

And while we are on the subject of open areas of swimming, children should be taught safety rules about boats and canoes. *They should remain seated while riding in them.* Another important rule is to stay with the boat if it capsizes, not try to swim back to the shore.

A young child such as we are dealing with here is not capable of rescuing another child, and must be taught that he should seek an adult if his buddy is in trouble, not try to make the rescue himself. There is too much chance of a double drowning.

And don't yell for help—go get it.

What all this boils down to is that even though children in this age group are very carefully supervised, *they should be taught the safety rules.* They aren't going to learn them by osmosis.

9

Fear

Fear is one of the most difficult problems we face in teaching swimming. Most children are not afraid of the water, but when you come across one who is, he must be dealt with very carefully, with tenderness and understanding. You can't talk him out of his fear, or tease him out of it, or bully him out of it. These things only make him more afraid. First, you must gain his confidence in you, and then you must help him to gain confidence in himself.

I said earlier that children in this age group learn more easily and have more fun if they learn in groups. However, this is not necessarily true of fearful children. These children need individual attention. And if a fearful child is put in a class of children who are learning very rapidly, it will only make him withdraw. Sometimes, though, by teaching two fearful children together, you will find they encourage each other. However, it doesn't always work out that way, because what one can't think of to be afraid of, the

74

other one can. Your approach should be entirely an individual matter when you're dealing with a fearful child.

In my opinion, fear should be dealt with frankly and openly. Talking about it, and explaining what fear is, will help a child overcome some of his anxiety. Many children are ashamed and feel guilty of being afraid, and such feelings add to their discomfort.

I explain to a fearful child that fear is Mother Nature's way of protecting us. If it weren't for fear, we'd get into a lot of dangerous situations and perhaps be harmed. We mostly are afraid of the unknown, I tell him, and a nonswimmer is afraid partly just because he doesn't know how to swim. As an example, I take an activity of which he is not afraid—perhaps riding a bike—and explain that he isn't scared of the bike because he knows how to ride, and that when he knows how to swim he won't be scared of the water, either. And then I explain that we all have fears—for example, I'm scared to death of horses. It makes a child feel more at ease knowing that fear is not peculiar to him alone.

So much for the generalities. Now let's get down to specifics. Most so-called fear isn't fear in the sense of outright terror, but apprehension, which is much easier to deal with.

For instance, I had a beginner group of five-year-olds at Black-Foxe School. The older boys on the swimming team, teasing them, told the youngsters they had put an alligator in the pool. I knew I wouldn't get anywhere denying it, so I said, "Sure, there's an alligator in there. His name is Serendipity, and he's magic. He can make himself disappear. Also he is very friendly, and if you see and touch him it will bring you good luck." So we spent a few days looking for Serendipity the alligator, and he soon became a part of the pool equipment.

Often a child will be afraid of trying a specific skill. One of the most common is floating. Perhaps he just can't let himself go and be suspended in the water. I help a child overcome this fear by letting him hold onto my arm while he is in the floating position. I encourage him to let go for just a second, then grab on again to my arm. Once he'll let go for just a second, I encourage him to let go for two seconds, three seconds, and so on. In no time at all he is floating on his own. In the beginning it is important for him to know that he can still grab onto your arm if he wants to.

Sometimes children will use "fear" to get attention. I once taught two brothers, ages five and six. The younger, Perry, was an outgoing, fun-loving character who wasn't afraid of anything. The older boy, Augie, was shy and introverted. The family and their friends gave Perry all the attention. When I saw what the situation was I began praising Augie to his younger brother and letting him demonstrate to Perry and his parents when he learned a new skill. Augie overcame his fear—when he got attention by *not* being afraid.

But now we come to the real "honest-to-gosh" deep-seated fear. I'm not talking about those spoiled brats who won't try—the "I don't have to" type. I mean children who get a look of horror on their faces when they put a big toe into the water. And as I said before, you can't tease them or shame them or bully them out of it.

After assuring such a fearful child that you understand and sympathize with him, tell him you will never force him to do anything he is unwilling to try, AND STICK TO IT. In this case, I think it's a good idea to keep your distance from the child and not touch him in any way, so that he won't get the idea that you are going to grab him and force him.

I usually start out by getting acquainted and establishing a rapport with a fearful child. Such rapport need not be associated with swimming. What's important is that he look on you as a friend and not some big ogre that he's in awe of.

(I admit I have an advantage because I'm very small, and a

child will more readily accept someone nearer his own size. To him a small person is young, a big person is old. Children think nothing of asking me my age, much to the horror of their parents, because they don't consider me an adult. I usually answer by asking them how old they think I am. And I've gotten some pretty funny answers. One little girl said, "Well, I'm seven and you're bigger than I am, but my brother is twelve and he's bigger than you, so I think you're eleven!" At Black-Foxe, flatteringly enough, one of the bigger fifteen-year-olds tried to date me!)

Anyway (sigh), back to the pool. I've found that praise and reward work wonders. Admittedly, praise is a kind of reward, but I use material rewards as well. A material reward is especially effective if it's something a child really wants. As I said before, I'm small, and I wear a shoe size three. I often reward a young girl with a pair of my old shoes for special accomplishments. You'd be surprised how hard a six-year-old girl will try for a pair of high-heeled shoes that fit. So find out, if you can, what a child really wants and use it as an inducement. And use praise very profusely with these fearful children, particularly in the beginning lessons. They'll discover that swimming is fun after all.

It is almost impossible to predict how long it will take a child to overcome his fear. Sometimes it takes months, even when you work with him several times a week. So you should start out with the idea that it will take some time, and if you happen to hit upon a quick solution to end his fear—consider yourself lucky.

But never forget how important it is to proceed slowly and with caution. When he is already afraid, it won't take much to create a deeper fear, which will only add to your problems.

10
Skills, Games, and Fun

Given the opportunity, children make up their own games in the water; but in organized play it's helpful to know several games for children in groups. Then, too, children can have more fun playing by themselves if they know certain skills. The mastering of skills in addition to the regular strokes helps make a better swimmer. The more maneuverability a swimmer has in the water the better swimmer he becomes.

Let's start with the skills that should be taught in the daily lessons as the child learns the strokes.

RETRIEVING OBJECTS FROM THE BOTTOM

Diving to the bottom of the pool to retrieve an object is one of the first skills I teach because it is one of the most popular. Be careful which objects you choose to use for recovering. I've seen rocks used, but I don't recommend them because children do throw things, even when they are told not to, and I think rocks are too dangerous. They can also be hard on feet if left beside the pool. This goes for ice-hockey pucks as well—or for anything else that could be injurious if thrown or ankle-wrenching if stepped on.

My own favorite is poker chips. The colored plastic ones are best because they are easy to see and easy to handle. Besides, they aren't dangerous if they are thrown. Of course money can be attractive—especially if children are allowed to keep the coins they recover! When I was training at the Riviera Club in Indianapolis, the whole swimteam was out bright and early every Monday morning to dive for coins that had been lost in the pool over the weekend by members of the club.

DIVING FROM THE SURFACE

Diving down into the water while already in it is technically known as a "surface dive." The trick is to get the head down and the feet up over the head. A common mistake that most beginners make is to kick their feet in trying to get down. When the head is down, the feet and legs will push the body down when they are up over the head. Kicking the feet makes it much more difficult. The theory behind it is this: The body or any part of it is heavier out of the water than it is in the water. Therefore, the half of the body that is in the water is lighter and the half out of the water is heavier. So the heavier feet and legs will move the arms and head down. Kicking the feet just stops the momentum.

To help a beginner get the "feel" of going down I give his head a push down a couple of times before he tries it on his own. After learning this skill, children like to stand and walk on their hands on the bottom of the shallow end of the pool.

The same theory holds true for the reverse skill of holding the arms up over the head and "sitting down" on the bottom of a shallow pool.

GOING DOWN IN DEEP WATER

Taking these two skills to the deep water leads to additional skills. When doing a surface dive in the deep water, a swimmer will often have to kick his feet to get to the bottom—but not until he is completely submerged and he begins to lose his momentum.

When going feet first in deep water, the swimmer holds his arms up over his head and "stands down" in the water instead of "sitting down" as he did in the shallow water. Of course, in deep water the likelihood of his getting to the bottom this way is almost nil, particularly if the water is more than seven feet deep. So, when he begins to lose his momentum, he starts kicking his feet and pulling up to the surface again.

SOMERSAULTS

Learning the skills of turning forward and backward somersaults is a lot of fun and helps a child develop better control of his body in the water.

The *forward somersault* is the easier of the two. Keeping the head forward and staying tucked up makes it simple to flip around in a circle. The *backward somersault* is a little more difficult but can be mastered by most children in this age group. The easiest method is to get the knees up to the chest and, with head back, rotate the arms at the side clockwise. Most of the difficulty is the inability of

Facing: Given the opportunity, children will make up their own games in the water.

the beginner to stay in the tuck position as he turns. If a child has too much trouble I hold him by the chin and pull him around so that he can get the feel of the motion.

Akin to somersaults is the skill of rolling over. Starting by floating on his back, the swimmer merely turns over—floating prone. He then continues over onto his back again. With practice he will soon be able to roll over and over, catching a breath whenever he is on his back. In learning this skill most children kick their feet as they try to roll over. But kicking makes turning much more difficult. The body and legs should be straight, with the hands at the sides. Rolling is quite an easy skill to learn.

TAG GAMES

Games take up a lot of the time that is spent in the pool, and I suppose tag games are the most popular. I strongly discourage tag games that require the participants to get out of the pool. No matter how many rules you make against it, children do get excited during a game and you just can't keep them from running—and, in general, disobeying other pool rules.

One tag game is a water version of "Blindman's Buff" called "Marco Polo." The person who is "it" stays at one end of the pool with his eyes closed; the others spread out in the pool. The game begins when the person who is "it" calls out "Marco" and the others answer "Polo." Then, with his eyes still closed, "it" tries to catch someone. Every time "it" calls out "Marco," the other players must answer "Polo." The first one caught is then "it."

Our little girl, Patty, adapted a game she learned in school to the pool. It's called "Uncle Sam." One person is "it" and stays in the middle of the pool. The others are lined up along one side of the pool. The object of the game is to get to the other side of the

82

pool without being caught. The children at the edge of the pool sing, "Uncle Sam, Uncle Sam, may we cross your river dam?" The leader answers, "Yes, you may; yes, you may—if you're wearing green today." Then those who are wearing green swim to the other side, trying not to get caught. If, however, one does get caught, he stays in the middle to help catch the others. Those who don't get caught wait on the opposite side of the pool as the game proceeds, with the leader calling out the different colors until all the children have had a chance to try to cross the "dam." The game continues with those in the middle trying to catch those swimming from side to side. The last one caught gets to be "it" next time.

There are, of course, lots of other tag games, but many are either too complicated or too difficult for children in this age group.

USING PLAY ACCESSORIES

Children love to play with inner tubes, racing in them or trying to upset each other. And a huge truck tube makes it possible to have a wonderful game of "King of the Mountain."

But a couple of words of warning about inner tubes are in order. First, a child shouldn't be allowed in an inner tube until he can swim well enough to protect himself if the tube deflates or overturns. Secondly, children should *never* dive through tubes. I know of a young boy who misjudged the opening while diving through a tube—and broke his neck.

Balls are always popular with children, in and out of the water. One use of the ball children enjoy is to see if they can catch a ball that is being thrown to them from someone standing on the edge of the pool as they jump off the diving board.

I often substitute a balloon for a ball. Partially filling a deflated balloon with water, and then blowing it up, makes a "ball" that is easier to handle than a regular one. Since we can't swim as fast as we run, the slower-moving balloon makes ball games more fun—particularly for this age group.

Speaking of balloons, filling them with water until they're only about the size of a baseball provides a lot of pleasure. They float just under the surface of the water, and children really enjoy playing with them.

A continuous game that can run for several weeks or months is a "Round-the-World Swim." This game encourages children to practice and is good for groups of varying ages and abilities.

Hang a world map poolside and scale the miles down to laps; each swimmer is identified on the map by a colored pin, then charts his path "around the world" as he progresses. The first one to get back to the original starting point, of course, wins.

These skills and games can be well accomplished by the average swimmer in this age group. Of course there are many more difficult skills that an extremely good swimmer can achieve, but for most participants they would be the exception and not the rule.

Children usually pick the skill or game that they like best and keep repeating it over and over instead of skipping from one to another. For instance, most children's favorite skill is diving for poker chips. And they most often choose a tag game for playtime. Also you'll probably find that they choose the same tag game each time, whether it is "Marco Polo" or something else. They don't play one game one time and another game another.

As I said at the beginning of this chapter, given the opportunity, children will make up their own games. I think you'll find that if you encourage them to do so, they will get more out of swimming—and have lots of fun doing it.

11
Review

Always when teaching children in this age group, you should keep several things in mind. First, I think it is important not to forget for one minute that they are learning so they can *enjoy* the water; therefore, the lessons should be fun. Always remember, too, that these children still have a rather short span of attention and the lessons shouldn't be one long laborious session, but a series of short exercises with skills. Children will try much harder to learn a given skill if they know that the lesson won't last long—particularly if it is a difficult skill for them to learn. Also, don't stick with one skill lesson after lesson.

For instance, once a child can do the hand-over-hand reasonably well, let him progress to the next skill of moving his arms while they are a half circle apart. From time to time, during other lessons, go back to practice the skills he began to learn earlier.

Always arrange time for play, so that a child will be able to spend part of the lesson period doing whatever he wishes in the water. This will not only give him a chance to learn new skills on his own, but will give you a control lever for discipline.

And, last, bear in mind that *a child's attitude toward swimming— good or bad—is greatly influenced by his parents and teacher.*

There was a little boy who had been given a pet turtle. When Mark came home from vacation he found the turtle dead. His father explained to him that the turtle would have to be disposed of; Mark became hysterical, and his father saw that he couldn't console him with words alone. So he said, "I'll tell you what, Mark, we'll give this turtle the biggest and best funeral any turtle ever had!" He made a coffin lined in red velvet and a special cross for the grave. Mark invited all the children in the neighborhood to the funeral, and they gathered flowers and planned a big procession. Just before the event got under way, Mark's father picked the turtle up to put it in the coffin—and it began to move. He called his son. Mark came running and said excitedly, "What, Daddy, what?" His father said, "I have some wonderful news for you, son. Your turtle isn't really dead after all—it was just hibernating. See, it moves."

Mark thought a minute and asked, "And we aren't going to have a big funeral and everything?" His father answered, "No, not now, and you'll have your turtle to play with again."

With that, Mark started crying and said, "Kill him, Daddy, kill him!"

You see? Your attitude counts for a lot, whatever you do.

So have fun!